IPAD PRO USER'S GUIDE

The Ultimate Tips and Tricks on How to Use Your iPad Pro in Best Optimal Way (2019 Update)

ALEXIS RODRÍGUEZ

Disclaimer

The information in this book is based on personal experience and anecdotal evidence. Although the author has made every attempt to achieve an accuracy of the information gathered in this book, they make no representation or warranties concerning the accuracy or completeness of the contents of this book. Your circumstances may not be suited to some illustrations in this book.

The author disclaims any liability arising directly or indirectly from the use of this book. Readers are encouraged to seek Medical. Accounting, legal, or professional help when required.

This guide is for informational purposes only, and the author does not accept any responsibilities for any liabilities resulting from the use of this information. While every attempt has been made to verify the information provided here, the author cannot assume any responsibility for errors, inaccuracies or omission.

TABLE OF CONTENTS

INTRODUCTION

The history of iPad dates back to 2010 when Steve Jobs was seeking to introduce a device that had features of both an iPhone and MacBook. The pioneering launch of iPad was a success as Apple Inc. was able to sell 3 million iPads within 80 days' time.

This made Apple launch a series of revolutionary iPads for the public. The original iPad Pro was introduced in 2015, consisting of the sweeping 12.9 inches display, 5.6 million pixels, four-speaker audio setup, 64-bit A9x chip, Smart Connector, and the innovative Apple Pencil.

This was followed by the compact iPad Pro 9.7, having a slender aluminum body along with Touch ID fingerprint sensor and striking rose gold color. It is much similar to the iPad Air 2 but with enhanced color saturation, Apple's pioneering True Tone Technology, and upgraded camera specifications.

Then came into the market was Apple iPad Pro 10.5 in the year 2017, which was launched to substitute iPad Pro 9.7 model. The new device was featured by a 20% bigger display and 40% condensed bezels. What made this model special was the A10x Fusion processor and the M10 motion co-processor, known for its 30% improved performance compared to the A9 and 40% better in graphics. People were provided an option to purchase state-of-the-art devices with great storage capacities including 64GB, 256GB, and 512GB.

Then the iPad Pro 11 was debuted in 2018, which offered a revamped design, squared edges, plunged bezels, advanced Face ID and lightning for USB Type-C

. Apart from this, iPad Pro was featured by the cutting-edge Liquid Retina Display, enhanced resolution, A12X Bionic Processor, 1 TB model, and upgraded cameras.

IPad Pro 11 was updated within the year of launch to iPad Pro 12.9 with some notable internal upgradations.

CHAPTER ONE

IPad Pro Technical Specifications

Models

Apple Inc. has launched its iPad Pro in five versions that include iPad Pro, iPad Pro 9.7, iPad Pro 10.5, iPad Pro 11 and iPad Pro 12.9.

Colors

Apple iPad Pro comes in two colors that include silver and space grey.

Capacity

IPad Pro first, second and third generations are available in 32, 64, 128, 256, 512 GB or 1 TB storage capacities.

Size and Weight

The recent iPad Pro 11 Wi-Fi model weighs approx. 460 grams. Whereas the upgraded model of iPad Pro 12.9 weights near to 630 grams. Both models are available in the Wi-Fi and cellular models with the same mass.

Button and Connectors

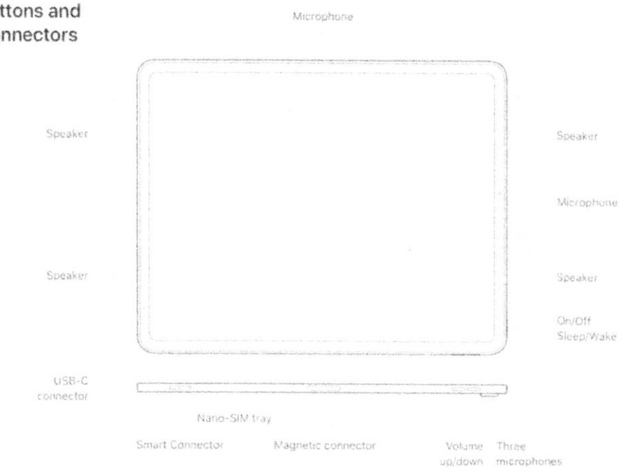

Display

IPad Pro offers the radical Liquid Retina Display having an 11-inches LED back-lit multi-touch presentation having IPS integrated technology.

- ProMotion feature
- Expanded-color display (P3)
- True Tone Display
- Fingerprint-resistant oleo phobic veneer
- Fully coated display
- Antireflective veneer
- More than 1.5% reflectivity
- 600 Nits illumination

IPad Pro models feature lovely curved designs.

Chip

IPad Pro features a powerful A12x Bionic chip which is incorporated with a neural engine and M12 co-processor.

Camera

IPad Pro comes with a twelve megapixel camera, a five element lens which can be zoomed up to five times. Users can also find Quad LED True Tone flash, Panorama that goes up to sixty three megapixels, azure crystal lens covering, rear lighting sensor, fusion IR filter, auto-focus with fixated pixels, animated photos with balance, eclectic shade apprehension for all kind of photos, enhanced local tone plotting, exposure regulator, noise tumbling, well-designed

HDR for photography, auto image equilibrium, torrent mode, timer approach, snap geotagging in all iPad Pro models.

Voice Recording

IPad Pro allows four thousand audio-visual footage, 1080p HD audio-visual footage at 30 fps or 60 fps and 720p HD audio-visual footage at 30 fps. The radical device comes with a Quad-LED True Tone flash, Slo-mo audio-visual support, time-interval audio-visual with equilibrium, film audio-visual equilibrium, unremitting autofocus film, noise diminishing, replay zoom, and video geotagging.

True Depth Camera

The True Depth Camera in iPad Pro is featured by 7-megapixel snaps, picture mode, picture lightning, Animoji and Memoji, 1080p HD film footage, Retina Flash with *f*/2.2 opening, varied shade apprehension for all kind of photos, smart HDR, rear brightness sensor, auto image equilibrium, torrent mode, exposure regulator and timer mode.

Video Calling

IPad Pro allows FaceTime video using Wi-Fi or cellular data.

Audio Calling

IPad Pro enables FaceTime audio with support of Wi-Fi or cellular data.

Speakers and Microphone

IPad Pro comes with 4-speaker audio, 5 microphones, visual footage along with audiotape.

SIM Card

When it comes to SIM card insertion, iPad Pro models are designed to incorporate Nano-SIM that supports Apple SIM6 and eSIM6

Location

All iPad Pro models include a digital scope, Wi-Fi connection, iBeacon micro position, Wi-Fi and Cellular models. The device is also supported by GPS, GLONASS, Galileo, and QZSS Cellular

Sensors

IPad Pro offers state-of-the-art Face ID to the users for added security. It also features a three-axis gyro, speedometer, indicator along with an ambient light radar.

FACE ID

The use of Face ID in iPad Pro is supported by the TrueDepth camera for face detection, and aids in unlocking the iPad, fortifying private data in apps and do procurements from the App Store, iTunes Store, and Apple Books.

Apple Pay

The iPad Pro users can pay in iPad application and on the web using the Face ID. They can also transfer and accept funds in communications.

Siri

iPad Pro users can make use of voices to direct messages, set prompts, attain practical recommendations, use headphones, and listen and categorize tunes.

Power, Battery, and Charging

IPad Pro models come with a USB-C port and power adapter which are used for charging purposes. The 11-inches iPad Pro model is operated by 29.37 watt per hour rechargeable lithium-polymer battery, whereas the 12.9-inches model has an integrated 36.71 watt per hour rechargeable same battery in 11-inch version.

Users can enjoy web browsing for a limit of ten hours, watch videos, listen to music and perform other tasks. Each iPad Pro model allows internet connectivity through Wi-Fi and cellular data and can enjoy nine hours of web-surfing by just using the cellular data network.

Operating System

IOS 12, is the globe's most special and protected device operating system, crammed with influential features that support the users to grab the most out of each day.

Accessibility

Accessibility is one of the amazing feature of Apple Phones. It assist individuals with frailties to use their iPad Pro with ease. Having provision for vision, audible range, corporal and knowledge and literateness incorporated in the iPad Pro, users can produce and perform remarkable things.

IPad Pro accessibility comes along with Voice Over, Siri, Transcription, Zoom, Assistive Touch, Switch Control, Magnifier, Locked Titles and Speak Screen.

Enable accessibility features on iPad.

1. From the Home screen, go to [Settings icon] and select **General**.
2. Select **Accessibility**.
3. Select and turn on the features you want to use.

In-Built Apps

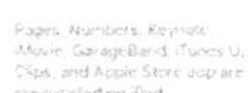

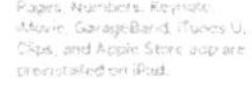

System Requirements

IPad Pro users require an Apple ID to use some features. It is important to have internet access to match with iTunes on a Mac or PC.

Supported Dialects

IPad Pro users have the following language support:

- English
- Chinese
- French
- German
- Italian
- Japanese

- Korean
- Spanish
- Arabic
- Catalan
- Croatian
- Czech
- Danish
- Dutch
- Finnish
- Greek
- Hebrew
- Hindi
- Hungarian
- Indonesian
- Malay

- Norwegian
- Polish
- Portuguese
- Romanian
- Russian
- Slovak
- Swedish
- Thai
- Turkish
- Ukrainian
- Vietnamese

Quick Type Keyboard Support

The Quick Type Keyboard Support for iPad Pro models include:

- English
- Chinese
- French
- German
- Italian, Japanese
- Korean
- Spanish
- Arabic
- Armenian
- Azerbaijani
- Belarusian
- Bengali
- Bulgarian
- Catalan

- Cherokee
- Croatian
- Czech
- Danish
- Dutch
- Emoji
- Estonian
- Filipino
- Finnish
- Flemish
- Georgian
- Greek
- Gujarati
- Hawaiian
- Hebrew

- Hindi
- Hinglish
- Hungarian
- Icelandic
- Indonesian
- Irish
- Kannada
- Latvian
- Lithuanian
- Macedonian
- Malay
- Malayalam
- Maori
- Marathi
- Norwegian

- Odia
- Persian
- Polish
- Portuguese
- Punjabi
- Romanian
- Russian
- Serbian
- Slovak
- Slovenian
- Swahili
- Swedish
- Tamil
- Telugu
- Thai

- Tibetan
- Turkish
- Ukrainian
- Urdu
- Vietnamese
- Welsh

IPad Pro Quick Type keyboard support with prognostic contribution include:

- English
- Chinese
- French
- German

- Italian
- Japanese
- Korean
- Russian
- Spanish
- Portuguese
- Thai
- Turkish

Siri languages

Siri in iPad Pro models offers the following languages:

- English
- Spanish

- French
- German
- Italian
- Japanese
- Korean
- Mandarin
- Cantonese
- Arabic
- Danish
- Dutch
- Finnish
- Hebrew
- Malay
- Norwegian
- Portuguese

- Russian
- Swedish
- Thai
- Turkish

Dictation languages

The dictation languages for iPad Pro device include:

- English
- Spanish

- French
- German
- Italian
- Japanese
- Korean
- Mandarin
- Cantonese
- Arabic
- Catalan
- Croatian
- Czech
- Danish
- Dutch
- Finnish
- Greek

- Hebrew
- Hindi
- Hungarian
- Indonesian
- Malaysian
- Norwegian
- Polish
- Portuguese
- Romanian
- Russian
- Shanghainese
- Slovakian
- Swedish
- Thai
- Turkish

- Ukrainian
- Vietnamese

Definition Dictionary Support

The definition dictionary support for iPad Pro include:

- English
- Chinese
- Danish
- Dutch
- French
- German
- Hebrew
- Hindi
- Italian

- Japanese
- Korean
- Norwegian
- Portuguese
- Russian
- Spanish
- Swedish
- Thai
- Turkish

Thesaurus

The thesaurus for iPad Pro is solely English of the United Kingdom and United States of America.

Multilingual dictionary support with English

IPad Pro users have an advantage for the multilingual dictionary support with English which entails the following:

- Arabic
- Chinese
- Dutch
- French
- German
- Hindi
- Italian
- Japanese

- Korean
- Portuguese
- Russian
- Spanish

Spell check

The spell check in the iPad Pro device accepts following languages:

- English
- French
- German
- Italian
- Spanish
- Danish

- Dutch
- Finnish
- Korean
- Norwegian
- Polish
- Portuguese
- Russian
- Swedish
- Turkish

Audio Playback

IPad Pro supports the following audio formats:

- AAC
- Protected AAC
- HE-AAC
- MP3
- MP3 VBR
- Dolby Digital
- Dolby Digital Plus
- Hearable setups 2, 3, 4, Traceable Enhanced Audial - AAX and AAX+
- Apple Lossless
- AIFF
- WAV
- User configurable extreme volume boundary

TV and Video

IPad Pro models include Airplay Paralleling, photographs, audial, and video out to Apple TV. It also ropes Dolby Vision and HDR10 content. The audio-visual paralleling and video out the support of up to 4000 through USB-C Digital AV multiport connector and USB-C VGA multiport connector.

Mail Support

The accessible document forms in iPad Pro include:

- .jpg
- . tiff
- .gif
- .doc

- .docx
- .htm and .html
- .key
- . numbers
- .pages
- .pdf (Preview and Adobe Acrobat)
- .ppt and .pptx
- .txt
- .rtf
- . vcf
- .xls
- .xlsx
- .zip
- .ics

Environmental Requirements

The Apple's iPad Pro can withstand an ambient temperature of up to 0° to 35° C. Besides this, the unacceptable temperature range includes –20° to 45° C. This device allows a virtual humidity of 5% to 95% non-condensing and operating altitude of up to 3000 meters.

CHAPTER TWO

An insight into iPad Pro Radical Accessories

IPad Pro series has introduced some revolutionary accessories for its valued users. Some of which are discussed in this chapter.

ACCESSORIES

SENSU ARTIST BRUSH AND STYLUS

Sensu Artist Brush and Stylus have replaced the use of finger to operate devices. This versatile accessory is known for having a two-ended stylus for creative hunts and is much economical compared to the Apple Pencil. It is also featured with a rubber stylus end and brush top which can be skilfully used as a navigation tool by the qualified artists due to its advantage of refashioning the feel of sketching on paper.

SATECHI BLUETOOTH MULTIMEDIA REMOTE

Satechi Bluetooth multi-media remote also known as a teeny remote tool has linked the gap between the TV and tablet. The new 12.9 inches iPad Pro resembles laptops for its ability to be doubled as great as a TV device. IPad Pro is also treasured because of the six months' battery life with a 33 feet signal scope it offers. Users can also regulate the media through volume control, navigation and other features of the iPad Pro.

AN EXCEPTIONAL LOGITECH SLIM FOLIO CASE WITH COMBINED WITH BLUETOOTH KEYBOARD

Logitech Slim Folio Case with Integrated Bluetooth Keyboard for iPad is best suited for businessmen to perform official tasks and even travelers for leisure activities. Its valuable features include well-spaced keys, built-in keyboard, and devoted iOS shortcut keys.

IPad Pro can prove highly useful for the people who are required to be at work all the time. The Logitech smart case with Bluetooth keyboard can effortlessly link with the iPad Pro for a swift setup, where the design supports the screen, typing, and browsing.

SANDISK IXPAND V2 USB FLASH

SANDISK IXPAND V2 USB FLASH offers enhanced storage for the iPad Pro, scaling it up to 128 GB. This facilitates users in storing a huge number of videos on the device, high-resolution photos, files with a supple connector to fit most situations. Users can watch videos directly from the device and is perfect for traveling situations where a disconnection occurs in trains and plane journeys.

The flash drive comes with a twin-ended USD drive and alleviating design.

The iPad Pro is known for being a valued portable dynamo which can be conveniently used for creative projects and other useful and leisure activities. The addition of some sensibly chosen accessories has made iPad Pro even much better choice for the users. Users can enjoy a productivity boost by using the radical Bluetooth keyboard which is slickly integrated into a folio case for travel purposes. There is a 1up civility of a wireless gaming regulator or a promotion to the big screen with support of an AV adapter. Creative users can enjoy the actual feeling of a paintbrush stylus, businessmen and pros can professionally perform their tasks on the go while other users have the chance to perform varied tasks.

CONNECTING A DIGITAL CAMERA

The recent iPad Pro model has marked history by incorporating a non-propriety charging berth i.e. USB-C port in replacement of lightning. This transformation is unfavorable to the people who owned bequest accessories. On the contrary, it is a huge advantage for the photographers as they can connect their digital camera into the iPad Pro and easily access images.

How to Connect?

The recent iPad Pro 2018 models are furnished with only USB-C which is not suitable for connecting a digital camera. So, to connect a camera one needs an adapter; the selection of an adapter depends on the type of camera being used.

Connecting a Digital Camera to an iPad Pro 2018

Digital camera usually has either a micro or mini USB port, which can easily be attached to the iPad with a single cable.

For iPad Pro, the users need to plug in mini-USB cable also.

SD Card

The easiest option to connect a camera to iPad Pro is through an SD card, which can conveniently be plugged in a USB-C adapter and eventually into the iPad Pro.

Proprietary Ports

Digital cameras with unique proprietary ports are challenging to handle, making USB-C to USB adapter the best choice. Although USB-C is a resourceful option, but surely a classy one also.

When users have the right accessories or kit, the remaining method is quite simple. The user is just required to connect the camera or SD card to the iPad Pro through appropriate cables or adapters. The Photo app in iPad Pro usually operates automatically, if this is not the case, one will have to open it manually and choose the import lab option.

CHAPTER THREE

Setting Up iPad Pro the Right Way

Setting up an Apple device is always a roller-coaster experience, and configuring an iPad Pro is even more electrifying.

Users need to know about the following things for setting up an iPad Pro:

Know Device Options

An iPad Pro can be configured through any of the following three methods:

Set Up as New: This implies setting up everything from scratch and is recommended for people who have not used Apple devices before or want a completely new look of their iPad.

Restore from Another Apple Device: This task is to be performed by users who have previously been using iOS devices and now want to add new iPad Pro to their collection. This is simple, all one needs is to perform this online using iCloud or USB with iTunes.

Import from Android: Apple has introduced a useful app 'Move to iOS' in Google Play for the Android device users, so they can conveniently switch to iPad Pro if they have been using other devices before.

How to configure the new iPad Pro?

When users switch on their new iPad Pro for the first time, they are welcomed by 'Hello' in various languages. This is the time when users need to decide whether to set up new, restore from another Apple device or import from Android.

To configure:

1. Users need to tap 'slide to set up' and glide the finger across the screen
2. Then users are required to choose their desired language

3. After this, the users are supposed to choose their country or region

4. Next, users need to select their Wi-Fi network. If Wi-Fi is not available, users can also choose the cellular option to connect to the internet.

5. If users want to set up their iPad Pro manually, they can follow the following steps:

o Tap 'Continue' after analyzing Apple's Data and Privacy information.

o Tap 'Enable Location Services' if the user wants to activate location services so that their position can be determined. If the user does not want to use the location services they can choose to 'Skip Location Services' and can enable location services later when setting up manually.

6. Following this, users can set up their Face ID

- Open Settings app
- Choose 'Face ID and Passcode'
- Enter Passcode
- Tap to set up Face ID
- Choose Get Started option
- The camera will appear, users need to aptly position their face inside the circle. Move swiftly in a circle and then in the second circle.
- Tap 'Done' option

7. After this, they can create a Passcode, through which they can set up a customary four-digit or six-digit passcode. On the contrary, they can

choose a personalized passcode by choosing the Passcode Options.

8. Then the iPad Pro will ask the user whether to restore data from backup, configure a new iPad or shift data from an Android device. Here is the way to restore or shift data from other devices:

Apple device users have two options when restoring data: iCloud and iTunes. Use of iCloud or iTunes depends on how the user has backed up the data in iCloud or via iTunes. Backing up an iPad is the most important and foremost thing.

To shift data from an Android device, users need to install the app 'Move to iOS' from the Google Play store, then follow instructions to accomplish the task.

Shifting from Android to iPad Pro

Here is what users need to do:

1. Choose 'Set Up as New iPad'

2. Enter Apple ID and Passcode. The users who do not have an Apple ID will have to choose 'Don't have an Apple ID' and follow instructions to do it.

3. Know and agree to Apple's terms and conditions

4. Again choose 'Agree' to validate

5. Configure Apple Pay

6. Configure iCloud Chain

7. Configure 'Siri' by calling out 'Hey Siri'

8. Choose to Send Diagnostic information to Apple when apps fail or any other issue arises. Users also have the option to not send if they don't wish to.

9. Go for 'Display Zoom' if the users want enhanced visual accessibility

10. Choose 'Get Started' option

CHAPTER FOUR

iPad Pro Software

SOFT AND HARD RESET

Apple allows hard and soft reset of their devices; users must know all particulars of resetting Apple devices. A hard reset erases all data and requires a backup. The users who have a lot of data on their phone are advised to perform soft reset before the hard reset.

Performing Soft Reset on iPad Pro

1. Users need to press and grip the Home and Power buttons simultaneously for almost 10 seconds and then release both. Apple logo will appear on the screen and the task is accomplished.

Performing Hard Reset on iPad Pro

Method 1: Rest through Settings

1. Open 'Settings'
2. Choose 'General'
3. Select 'Reset'
4. Tap 'Erase all content and settings'

Method 2: Reorganize through iTunes

1. Connect the iPad to the MacBook or PC
2. Open iTunes
3. Choose the iPhone icon and circumnavigate to Summary

4. Tap 'Restore iPhone' button

5. Users will receive a message after tapping the restore iPhone button.

6. Tap 'Restore and Update' button to accomplish hard reset

Method 3: Retune through DFU Mode

1. Switch off iPad Pro

2. Join iPad to the computer system

3. Open iTunes

4. Press and grip the "Power" and "Home" buttons simultaneously for about 10 seconds

5. Wait for 10 seconds, discharge the power button and carry on pressing the home button for 10 more seconds.

6. A message pop-up will appear after this on the computer screen

7. Go to iTunes and tap Restore iPhone button

iPadOS

iPadOS has been formed under the same basis as iOS, with the addition of some innovative competences and in-built features specific to the resourcefulness of the iPad Pro.

iPadOS has presented ground-breaking ways to work with apps in many windows, reformed Home screen, customary ways to use Apple Pencil, upgraded software iOS 13, which makes it highly suitable for creative users, professionals and the public. Users can suitably use the advanced tool palette, colors, and shapes through the use of the state-of-the-art Apple Pencil.

New Home Screen

IPad Pro offers a new Home screen with a reformed layout that is able to accommodate more apps on the screen. Users also have to option to add 'View' to the Home screen, permitting swift access to widgets for an instant glimpse at the info.

Work more with Split View and Slide Over

iPad Pro users are able to work with several files and documents at the same time, by using the same app through the new split view feature. They can also swiftly view and shift between several apps in the Slide Over.

Other ways to Use Apple Pencil

iPad OS has made the use of Apple Pencil more facilitated than ever. Users are now able to chalk up and lead complete webpages, documents or emails on the iPad Pro by just swiping the Apple Pencil. The radical Apple Pencil offers innovative prediction algorithm and optimizations to condense its industry-leading potential to as little as 9 milliseconds.

Powerful Files App

iPadOS had made files app (a hub that allows smooth access and management of documents) improved by the support of iCloud Drive. The new software also supports external drives, permitting users to conveniently plug-in USB drives, SD cards and sign in to SMB file through the files app. The local storage, new keyboards shortcuts along with zipping and unzip feature are included in the iPadOS.

Desktop Browsing Experience with Safari

iPadOS mechanically presents the desktop form of the website, which has been adjusted according to the iPad Pro screen. Users also have the advantage of using significant new features like download manager, keyboard shortcuts and tab management.

Enhanced Text Editing

iPadOS has made text editing advanced through a significant update, thus making it convenient, swifter and precise.

More iPadOS Features

- Dark Mode
- Custom Fonts
- Floating Keyboard and support for QuickPath
- Photos Curates
- Faster Sign in with Apple to apps and websites
- Maps Feature
- Presentation Screen

CHAPTER FIVE

Why is iPad Pro Special?

iPad Pro offers the pioneering all-screen design and next-generation performance. The radical iPad Pro models feature an 11-inches and 12.9 inches Liquid Retina Display and incorporate state-of-the-art Facial ID to safely unravel iPad with just a glimpse.

iPad Pro also has the pioneering A12x Bionic chip integrated with a next-generation Neural Engine and apps which outstrips many PCs and laptops. The USB-C connector, Gigabit-class LTE, 1TB storage and the multi-touch screen has made the device suitable for versatile users.

The exceptional second-generation Apple Pencil in iPad Pro fascinatingly attributes to the iPad Pro with the best ever wireless charging. The pioneering touch sensor on the Apple Pencil presents a completely new approach for the apps.

The innovative Smart Keyboard Folio comes along with a modernized design that can be accustomed to enhanced resourcefulness. Thus, iPad Pro shows that Apple has taken a great step towards the influential and inspired mobile computing as it offers the revolutionary slender design and accelerates through super-fast A12x Bionic chip, state-of-the-art Face ID, Smart keyboard Folio, advanced camera and sensors ensuring superlative AR experiences, speedy USB-C connector, powerful battery, strong speakers and the pioneering Apple Pencil.

Design and Screen

iPad Pro is known for featuring the most advanced Liquid Retina display along with the precision-milled glass, cutting-edge pixel covering, sub-pixel antialiasing and the original backlight design. iPad Pro has the truest color iPad display that offers a True Tone and anti-reflective veneer to ensure a usual, precise viewing experience.

The ProMotion technology mechanically regulates the display refresh rate of up to 120Hz for a highly suave scrolling and improbable sensitivity of iPad Pro. The all-new 11-inches iPad Pro version offers a huge display with enhanced pixels compared to the other 10.5-inches model. And the 12.9-inches iPad Pro model offers the major display into a handy package, making it convenient to be carried anywhere.

A12x Bionic Chip

The new iPad Pro model is the reediest laptop ever, having a thickness of just 5.9 mm. The A12x Bionic chip has been built explicitly for the iPad Pro making the device highly smart and powerful.

Planned particularly for the iPad Pro, A12x Bionic is the well-designed and influential chip ever, efficiently facilitating the commonest computer tasks. Based on the leading seven-nanometre technology, the influential A12x Bionic includes four performance and four competence interiors for a flawless single core performance. It also comes with an original performance regulator for concurrent use of all cores for 90% enhanced experience during the multi-threaded jobs.

GPU

The seven-core, Apple GPU ensures double visuals performance for amazingly rich AR experiences and support-quality visuals. iPad Pro is distinguished for the advance, long-lasting and powerful performance. Apple's innovative Neural Engine has been incorporated for progressive machine learning which allows swift Face ID and level detection. This feature also allows boosted recital for Core ML tasks and workflows that employ extremely competent machine learning engine.

Face ID

iPad Pro users have a great advantage of safe facial verification system – the Face ID, which can be used in any possible way using the pioneering Smart Keyboard Folio. Face ID being duly supported by the TrueDepth camera, enables iPad Pro face recognition to safely access the phone, Apple Pay and other apps.

Innovative Apple Pencil and Nifty Keyboard Folio

The second-generation Apple Pencil gracefully ascribes to the iPad Pro, making it highly suitable for the highly artistic and prolific users through the nifty keyboard folio it offers. The smart Keyboard Folio which features a modernized and versatile design is best suited for multitasking and imaging down thoughts.

The gains of USB-C

The incredible and multipurpose USB-C type of connector has aptly substituted the lightning connector that is al. USB-C ropes in USB 3.1 Gen 2 for high-bandwidth data transmissions ensuring double speed along and external displays. With the support of adaptable USB-C, the iPad Pro can also assist in charging a phone.

iOS 12 is now available with iPad Pro

iPad Pro users can also enjoy the perks of iOS 12 through powerful and automated workflows and multitasking. Group FaceTime in iPad Pro is another revolutionary feature that has made connecting with friends and associates unbelievably easy. The Animoji and personalized Memoji allow users to take benefit of the big screen

CONCLUSION

Apple has improved its 10.5-inch iPad Pro and taken that to the next level with an exemplary display and exceptional performance. You would definitely be mesmerized to see the all-new huge display in the same size and weight. It's not just another hardware it brings some exceptional advantages along when it comes to app support. You can find numerous application that has been specifically designed to run well on the iPad which is something that is hard to find in other tablets.

Looking upon all the facts and figures the only competition that Apple iPad has its own sibling the 12.9inch model. Despite being similar in all the specifications it comes with a larger display and a higher price tag. Those who are looking for an iPad that brings them all those advantages with a compact design then they must go for the 10.5 inch iPad pro over its sibling competitor because of it compact yet powerful and also comes with an affordable price tag.

ABOUT THE AUTHOR

Alexis Rodriguez belongs to a group of Tech editorial team and is already testing the echo loudspeaker before its market launch. Gathering experience with innovative Ambient Assisted Living devices while studying and blogging about it for many years. In addition, in 2017 he wrote the first comprehensive overview of Alexa compatible devices.

Vacuum robots, smart home cameras and remote-controlled garden tools are also among his favorite subjects today.

INDEX

M

N

O

P

Q

R

S

T

U

V

W

Z

Made in the
USA
Middletown, DE

74606555R00056